Simon Vinnicombe

City Love

GW00391620

B L O O M S B U R Y
LONDON · NEW DELHI · NEW YORK · SYDNEY

Bloomsbury Methuen Drama

An imprint of Bloomsbury Publishing Plc

50 Bedford Square	1385 Broadway
London	New York
WC1B 3DP	NY 10018
UK	USA

www.bloomsbury.com

Bloomsbury is a registered trade mark of Bloomsbury Publishing Plc

First published 2013

British Library Cataloguing-in-Publication Data
A catalogue record for this book is available from the British Library.

ISBN: PB: 978-1-4725-3402-6
ePub: 978-1-4725-2950-3
ePDF: 978-1-4725-2881-0

Library of Congress Cataloging-in-Publication Data
A catalog record for this book is available from the Library of Congress.

Typeset by Country Setting, Kingsdown, Kent CT14 8ES
Printed and bound in Great Britain

City Love

Simon Vinnicombe

City Love
received its world premiere at
the CLF Art Cafe, Bussey Building
in Peckham Rye on 10 September 2013.

It was directed by Sarah Bedi
for The Orange Line Collective
and was supported by the National Lottery
through Arts Council England.

Cast

Ian Bonar – Jim

Theatre credits include: *Brilliant Adventures* (Manchester Royal Exchange); *Me, As a Penguin* (Arcola Theatre); *Beauty and the Beast* (Told by an Idiot/Lyric Hammersmith); *DNA* (National Theatre); *The Miracle* (National Theatre); *Ma Vie en Rose* (Young Vic); *Flat Stanley* (West Yorkshire Playhouse); Phillip Pullman's *Aladdin* (Bristol Old Vic); *Anorak of Fire* (Diorama Studio).

Film credits include: *Jack Ryan* (dir. Kenneth Branagh); *Skyfall* (dir. Sam Mendes); *Kon-Tiki* (dir. Joachim Rønning and Espen Sandberg); *Tintin* (dir. Steven Spielberg); *1234* (dir. Giles Borg); *How to Lose Friends and Alienate People* (dir. Robert B. Weide); *Atonement* (dir. Joe Wright); *Starter for Ten* (dir. Tom Vaughan).

Television credits include: *Black Mirror, Southcliffe* (Channel 4); *Going Postal* (Sky); *Holy Flying Circus, Hotel Babylon, New Tricks* (BBC); *Scott & Bailey, Secret Diary of a Call Girl, Teenage Kicks* (ITV); *Kabadasses* (E4).

Natasha Broomfield – Lucy

Theatre credits include: *Prophesy* (Blackall Studios); *Chariots of Fire* (Hampstead Theatre/West End); *Anne and Zef* (Salisbury Playhouse); *13* (National Theatre); *Electra* (Gate Theatre/Young Vic); *Greenland* (National Theatre); *Ghosts* (Arcola Theatre/ATC); *Fiddler on the Roof* (West End/Sheffield Theatre); *Diamond* (King's Head Theatre); *Men Should Weep* (Oxford Stage Company).

Television credits include: *Holby City, The Worst Week of My Life, Stacey Stone* (BBC).

Natasha was a runner-up in the Carlton Hobbs Awards.

Creative Team

Simon Vinnicombe – Writer

Simon won a Peggy Ramsay Pearson Award in 2010 and was a member of the BBC Writers Academy. He is currently on commission for Soho Theatre and the National Theatre.

Theatre credits include: *Show Me the World* (Underbelly, Edinburgh, 2011); *Cradle Me* (Finborough Theatre, 2008); *Wisdom* (Manhattan Theatre Club, New York, 2008); *Turf* (Bush Theatre, 2008); The 24 Hour Plays (Old Vic, 2007); *A Night with the Apathists* (Union Theatre, 2006); *Year 10* (Finborough Theatre, 2005) – Time Out Critics' Choice; *Wilde Tales* (Southwark Playhouse, 2005).

Radio credits include: *Mary Cherry*, *Hard Road* (BBC Radio 4, 2007).

Sarah Bedi – Director

Directing credits include: *Prophesy* (nominated for Best Ensemble at the Off West End Awards, 2013); *Macbeth* (Nominated for Best Director, Best Production, Best Ensemble and Best Sound Design at the Off West End Awards, 2011) for Baz Productions; *SEN Festival 2012* for the Young Vic; *Iphigenia at Aulis* for the Year Out Drama Company.

Assisting credits include: *Larisa and the Merchants* for InSite Performance at the Arcola.

Sarah is resident director and co-founder of Baz Productions for whom she will be directing *A Dream Play* in 2014.

Zanna Mercer – Designer

Recent theatre design and construction credits include: *Short Cuts III: A Box of Tricks* (Hen & Chickens Theatre, 2013); *Freedom, Books, Flowers and the Moon* (Waterloo East Theatre, 2012) and *The Inappropriateness of Love* (Hen & Chickens Theatre, 2012), both for Paradigm Theatre Company.

Other theatre credits include: *Ondine* (White Bear Theatre, 2012); *Glam Rock Murder Mystery* (Amersham Arms, 2012); *As Fate Would Have It . . .* (Etcetera Theatre, The Space, Lion and

Unicorn Theatre, 2011); *Play* and *I'm Not Waving* (Between Spaces: Live Art Festival, Goldsmiths, 2011); *Hitting Town* (White Bear Theatre, 2011); *The Nutcracker* (Pentameters Theatre, 2010); *Feathers* (White Bear Theatre and C Venues, 2010); *Shape* (George Wood Theatre, Goldsmiths, 2010); *A Midsummer Night's Dream* (Network Theatre, 2009); *The Tempest* (George Wood Theatre, Goldsmiths, 2009); *H1N1* and *Mistakes in the Background* (both Studio, Goldsmiths, 2009)

Commercial credits include: event design and management for Unilever and Molton Brown.

Anna Landreth Strong – Producer

Credits for exhibitions and events include: *Music Hall: Sickert and the Three Graces* (V&A, 2013); *Transformation and Revelation: Gormley to Gaga – UK Design for Performance* (V&A, 2012); *The House of Annie Lennox* (V&A/UK tour, 2011); *Five Truths*, directed by Katie Mitchell (V&A, 2011); *A Flash of Light: The Dance Photography of Chris Nash* (V&A/UK tour, 2011). Anna works at the V&A as Assistant Curator of Modern and Contemporary Performance and as an Exhibitions and Events Coordinator for the Department of Theatre and Performance. Upcoming projects for the V&A include work with the RSC, National Theatre, Globe and Fifty Nine Productions.

Other credits include: *Jumping and Other Thoughts* (Underbelly, Edinburgh, 2008), *Have You Seen Enough Yet?* (Workshop Theatre, Leeds, 2008).

Kat Gagan – Stage Manager

Theatre credits include: *Into the Little Hill* (Snape Maltings); *Miss Julie* (BAC); *Numbers* (Etcetera Theatre); *Slay it with Music* (Space Docklands, Greenwich Playhouse); *Chasing Shadows* (Camden People's Theatre); *Hansel and Gretel* (King's Head Theatre); *Ondine* (White Bear Theatre); *Unknown/Small Chances* (Leicester Square Theatre); *Paradise Street* (St John's Crypt); *Trash* (The Space, White Bear Theatre); *Freedom, Books, Flowers and the Moon* (Waterloo East Theatre); *33% Festival* (Oval House Theatre); *Tartuffe* (Canal Café Theatre); *Larisa and the Merchants* (Arcola Theatre).

Event credits include: *Brief Encounter, Bugsy Malone* (Future Cinema at the Troxy).

Film credits include: *The Fitting* (Central Film School).

WWW.ACORN.LTD.UK

WE

SE15

28 PECKHAM RYE - LONDON - SE15 4JR

he Heart of Residential Sales & Lettings in SE15

020 7771 6777

The Acorn Group

acorn LANGFORD RUSSELL John Payne UNIQUE MAP sta

The Orange Line Collective

would like to thank some very special people who generously gave their time, advice and creativity to the production (oh, and a bed). There are too many to thank here, but we'll try, in no particular order . . .

Simon Vinnicombe

Mickey Smith, Lucca Joy Barratt, Saija Kamarainen and all the staff at the CLF Art Cafe

Becky Wootton and staff at the Royal Court Theatre

Sam Smith and Cassandra Mathers of the Pleasance Theatre

Dulcie Alexander of Southwark Council

Emma Luffingham of BAZ Productions

Rowan Rutter (Creative Producer)

Christina Cooke of Gordon and French

Oliver Slinger and Natalie Day of Independent Talent

Nick Quinn of The Agency

Neil McPherson of the Finborough Theatre

Simon Darwen

Mark Weinman

And not forgetting . . .

Ben, Cathy, Anne and David Bedi

David, Christine and Frances Landreth Strong

Carol, Peter and Polly Misch

Sophie Holden

Jack Wilkinson

We are also grateful to our supporters

Arts Council England

Acorn Ltd

The Co-operative Membership Community Fund

Sheila Hancock CBE

Sir Tom Stoppard

Sam Adamson

Melanie Langer

Acknowledgements

I have an awful lot of people to thank for helping me over the course of writing this play. Thank you to Sarah Bedi and Anna Landreth Strong for your brilliant and tireless work, you are the reason this play is happening. And to Nick Quinn for such wonderful support and guidance over many years.

I would like to thank all of the staff of the Evelina Children's Hospital for saving my son's life and for continuing to care for him in a way that overwhelms me every second of every hour, every day. To Meisha Costa, Jon Lillie, Megan Wasserfall, Barbara Widmer, Dr Tony Hulse, you have changed my life. I'll never get close to saying thank you properly and I will never shut up about the extraordinary work you do. Much more than staggering professionalism, empathy in spades, support by the bucket load and remarkable human kindness. Thank you.

My son George, I can't type a word without dissolving into a puddle of tears. Look into my eyes any time, day or night. You know. Love. And your baby sister, Ava, teach her all that you've taught me and love her the way only you can. You two are the light.

Massive thanks to Wallace, Julie, Roger, Stephen, Tom, Susie, Helena, Ilia, Sophie, Minnie, Alex and Raphy Vinnicombe. And to the remarkable Anna Harris, we love you very much.

Simon Vinnicombe
July 2013

City Love

This play is for my wife.
There's nothing without you.
Thank you for George and Ava.
Happy here. Happy now.

Characters

Lucy
Jim

§

indicates the passing of time or place

Act One

Lucy *is sitting in a chair addressing someone. Dressed for work.*

Lucy   I didn't want a boyfriend at all. I don't want excitement or giddiness. Or tumbling bellies and tingly toes. I wake with clarity.

And that's fine.

Okay to good job. Good flat in okay-to-bad area.

And it's mine. Well. Rented. But.

Jim *creeps out of the darkness, tired and dishevelled.*

Jim   A room.

Lucy   Ikea furniture. Exposed brickwork. Lots of bleached wood and white upholstery. A silver coffee machine that gleams and hums.

Jim   A room in my sister's flat.

It's split level. Well. My room is in the basement. My sister with a proper job. And a pension.

Lucy   I don't use the machine. I like to walk into work with a coffee in a paper cup from the organic place round the corner. It makes me look like I'm in a rush. Like a woman with a career in the middle of a dazzling social life.

Jim   Because who can afford to live anywhere else. And who am I supposed to live with? Gumtree mates?

I can't live somewhere that I'm frightened to walk into the living room.

At my age I'm supposed to be moving up from somewhere I don't like. Somewhere alien, unattractive and slightly terrifying.

But pass off this place as cool.

'Elephant and Castle'.

'Archway'.

'Deptford'.

Moving to somewhere I really can't afford. With stripped-wood flooring. With a girlfriend. With fresh done highlights. And a boarding school history.

To 'Clapham'.

I'm not supposed to be in a sibling's basement.

Lucy   I live alone. It pushes me to the limit with my wages but it means I'm independent and not a girl who could be in a sitcom. A real woman.

Jim   I don't have any mates I could live with. Not without us being mistaken as a disappointed couple.

Lucy   Some friends. Not many but one good one who rings. Kim. She's funny and knows lots of cool people and places.

The city opens out when I'm with her.

§

Jim *now lit only by his open laptop.*

Jim   Loneliness doesn't cut it. You don't have any idea of who you are as a person until you're accepted by another.

And I was for a while.

I begin conversations with women and walk away before the bad bit. When she'll ask what I do. Or where I live. Or if I drive. Or if I'm eighteen grand in debt. Or if I own more than my bed at the age of twenty-nine and cry at least once a week when I try and go to sleep.

Lucy   I don't go out to talk to men. It's not what I go out for. This isn't a place you should be owned.

Jim   I check my email at work over three hundred times a day in the hope that one might arrive that improves my life.

But they're all about blue pills and people offering to improve my life by giving me a penis enlargement.

I haven't had the chance to know if the penis is the problem.

Lucy   Drink in bars with no signs on the door. Bars in boutiques. Bars in basements. On rivers and canals and roofs and on top of giant great bloody skyscrapers. With people from all over the world. And everyone has made the decision to be there.

Jim   Meet friends in crowded bars. We stand and pretend to scout for women and try and have conversations in crushed single file.

Go to clubs and look at women who we are too scared to ever utter a word to.

Lucy   Every meeting is a new possibility. Everything is in flux.

Jim   Everyone seems to be going somewhere here. Going to be something or somebody. Working in a job where they earn more money for people who are already rich. I want to say 'Well done you!' (*Sarcastic.*)

But they all seem so sure about how brilliant it is.

I'm sure about nothing. I've taken to lying about my future. Making one up. I can start to talk about 'Doing the thing I love' (*forced jollity*) but I shrivel into the ground before they ask me too many questions about how exactly that's going. There doesn't seem to be anything as shameful as having no life-plan in the city.

He folds into himself on the floor. He begins to toss and turn as if in his sleep.

Lucy   In four years I'd expect to be a senior buyer. I'd like to run my own department. Transform it. Lead.

In seven years I could be looking at planning for a family. Three years out. Back to work. Six years. Hard at it. And I could retire.

I couldn't last for ever in the city. One day the party has to stop. Retreat to the country and read.

Jim   I text three people this week. One was to vote for a TV show. One was my duty manager and one was my sister, who didn't respond.

I'm supposed to have friends. I'm supposed to be having the time of my life.

My face is wrong.

I wore the wrong clothes.

§

Lucy *enters carrying a glass of champagne. She looks out.*

Lucy   I walk across Waterloo Bridge every morning and the city seems like a playground.

Last night we went to an exhibition in a room with a glass wall hanging over the Thames. All those lights shining on the river look like fairy lights and disco balls. The whole city looks like a dazzling concrete party.

Jim   I'm sat on my arse playing on a video console in the dark. Or wanking to internet porn. And then I'll catch a glimpse of myself.

He slams his laptop shut.

§

Lucy   This seems like a place you can re-emerge. I love that.

I didn't want to sit around reading song lyrics again on the internet. Wallowing in sadness. My sadness. Other people's sadness. I'd stopped doing that.

Jim (*in darkness*)   You can feel as if you're disappearing through the cracks here. And no one would know you were gone.

Lucy   A heart doesn't mend. John is still . . .

But you can try and run away. Here you can run from anything.

She sings the first verse of 'Save Me'.[1]

Can't believe I did that. What am I?

§

Jim *is dressing himself for work.*

Jim   I'm not from the city. It's a shock when you take your first steps here.

It's a brutal, cruel, violent, ugly place. People don't like each other. They don't mix unless they're trying to sell each other something.

Can't walk down the street without being accosted by an overly smiling face attached to a clipboard, asking for a moment of your time. And virtually rugby-tackling you into the gutter.

I once grew a pair of balls and approached a beautiful woman in a shopping mall. I was about to ask her out. For a drink. I thought carefully about the right thing to say. I looked her in the eye. 'Excuse me,' I said. But before I could say anything more she told me I could stick my kick-boxing classes up my arse.

How are you supposed to meet someone in a place like that?

§

Lucy *leans forward on her chair.*

Lucy   I don't think it helps to talk about when we first met.

I just don't think it helps.

I'm here to talk about what's wrong.

She sits back again. Relents.

---

[1] Words and music by Brian May

Fine.

Fine.

On a bus.

Night bus.

Jim (*stands*)   A mixture of fried chicken and the drunken bile of the rejected men fills the air. A sort of 'noisy forced jollity with undercurrent of violence'. Don't make eye-contact. With anyone. At any point.

Lucy   Being on one of those is an act of survival. Men usually stare at you. Like you're some kind of prey. One had sat down next to me. Completely empty at the time. He sits next to me.

And he starts brushing his hand against my leg. Not obviously. Just the back of his hand on my leg. Not enough so I feel I can say anything. I think about moving seats but will it make a scene. Does that mean he'll talk to me? Do you know what I mean?

This happens a lot. Once I was stood up in a packed bus. The doors opened at a stop. A man just grabbed my breasts and then jumped off laughing.

I should get a taxi but who can afford a taxi? A proper taxi as opposed to a promise of mild to aggressive sexual harassment from a non-English-speaking lunatic in a Datsun.

Jim *takes the empty chair. Sits opposite* **Lucy**.

A brief moment. He clocks her.

Lucy   I feel his eyes on me. When you can just feel someone watching you. And for some reason I look up.

Jim *looks away. Does a good job of covering his embarrassment.*

Lucy   He looks out the window. As if he's deep in thought.

He's well dressed with round eyes that look soft and kind. His whole body looks relaxed into the floor. His clothes are nice.

He looks clean.

He's on the edge of smiling all the time.

You don't talk to people here. Not in the city. So I just . . .

Okay. Now I want him to look at me. Feel bad when he doesn't. Start to think about reasons why he's not looking at me any more. Look down at my clothes.

The dress I'm wearing shows a bump on my belly. My black tights make my legs look like lumpy trunks. The lights are so bright on these bloody things!

Jim *looks at* **Lucy** *again. He does all the following . . .*

Lucy We make eye contact. Then again. And again. I feel a little excited. The corners of his mouth almost make a smile.

Then he starts to play with his phone.

You arrogant prick. He's playing with me.

And then he laughs to himself as he reads something on his phone. I think he might be a little in love with himself. Knowing I'm watching him. And.

Then.

I get off the bus.

She leaves. **Jim** *looks devastated.* **Lucy** *speaks out front again.*

Lucy I have to get another one to get to Peckham Rye.

Feel embarrassed. I put myself up for sale for a few minutes and he didn't want to buy.

Fucking tights.

She returns to sitting opposite **Jim***.*

Jim I think my teeth got stuck on my lips when I tried to smile. Always happens when I'm nervous.

So I don't want to smile.

When I do it's a half of one. Sort of. Half leering. Half. Moron.

Can't work out if she's looking at me or looking where the bus is going. She fiddles with the back of a hair in her finger and thumb. Looks like she's thinking about something else. Someone else.

Girls like confidence, don't they?

I feel hot. Bit sweaty. Not in a sexy way.

Wow.

Fuck me. She's so pretty. Oh my God, she's just . . .

Why is it that every time I try and look cool I just come across as a complete prick?

For the first minute or so I'm okay at not talking. But then it becomes a failure.

I'm bottling it again.

What's the worst that can happen?

. . . She gets off the bus.

Lucy *goes.*

Jim   And she's gone.

I look around the bus and *everyone* else knows.

Even the driver knows.

That I am an apology for a human being.

Back to my hole in the city where no one can see me. Back to non-living. Back to . . .

No.

At the next stop . . .

I get off the bus. And I run back towards the previous stop. I'm overcome with a sense to see her again.

Which almost vanishes as I get close.

He is looking at **Lucy** *sitting at a bus stop.*

Jim   She's sat there. With her arms crossed, waiting for another bus. The light from the shelter shines down on her cheeks. Those eyes. Her hair. Her tights-clad legs crossed over one another as she sits. So perfectly. So. Wow.

I suddenly get a feeling that she's far too good for me.

I've got no right talking to her. I don't have any words to say.

He says the following to **Lucy**.

Jim   I don't have a place of my own.

I don't earn any money.

My sister still gives me money because I'm not man enough to do it on my own.

And I've only had sex with two women.

Badly.

And I cried three times last week on the bathroom floor and I don't know why.

But I have to talk to her.

Have to say hello.

(*To* **Lucy**.) Hello.

And she looks down. Then looks back up again. And she smiles.

Wow. Wow. Wow.

Jim *goes.*

§

Lucy *retreats to her bed.*

She looks at her phone. She deliberates. Decides against it. Puts her phone in her pocket.

She starts to ready herself for work. She's meticulous in her preparation. Fixes her hair up. Puts her glasses on. Straightens her clothing. She takes a clothes brush and brushes her suit jacket.

She looks at herself in the mirror.

She starts to cry.

§

Jim   She's not rung for two days now.

A normal person brushes this off and strides on. When I was thirteen and waiting for Natalie Bridstock to ring the phone at least I could lie to myself that she was trying to ring but my mum was on the line.

Now I've got this stupid fucking BlackBerry. It pings every time I get an email, or a text and.

Was it my hair?

Was it my face?

Did I wear the wrong clothes?

Girls don't think about boys like me.

I'm in no one's dreams.

Turn the phone on silent and then find myself checking the phone every minute to see if . . .

The rejection feels shameful. Like something I should own up to. I mean.

I tell Tony at work. He laughs. Feel better for telling someone. Relief when rejection is public.

'Fuck her, mate' was his sound advice. It's left his head before it ever got there. But for me . . .

§

Lucy   I don't want to ring him. I don't want to speak to him.

But I think about it every minute of every day. I think about him.

Frightened of what comes next.

She stares down at her phone. She gazes at it as though it were almost an instrument of torture.

I believe in preparation. It's what I do very well at work.

So I will just write things to say on the phone. In case I get a bit stuck or the conversation doesn't flow or my mouth dries and I feel like an eight-year-old kiss-chaser who doesn't know how to talk to a boy.

She starts to write things down on a pad.

(*Writes.*) 'What you been up to this week?'

'Have you been talking to any strange women in bus stops lately' . . . That's even less funny written down.

'I thought I'd ring.'

Oh dear lord!

No.

She starts typing on her phone.

I decided . . . that I couldn't get enough words in a text . . . and more than one text always seems a little bit . . . needy.

She smiles. Pleased with that. Continues to type.

Get nervous on the phone and never say anything I want to.

An email can be drafted and still come out this bad!

I had a lovely time the other night . . . I'm sorry I've taken two days to respond. My friends had a big talk to me about the number of days I should wait to respond . . . There was no consensus . . . other than ringing you the next morning would make me a bunny boiler with no life. I don't understand any of this by the way!

You should know that I wanted to ring you the minute you walked away from the bus stop.

My friends will kill me for telling you that.

So . . . In short . . . I'd like to go out with you sometime. Very much.

The only problem with email now is how to sign off.

On the phone is that I'd just say bye . . . This is the come-uppance for the coward I suppose. So I'm not going to put love, because I don't do that for my mum . . . I'm going to go with two kisses. After all we've only just met . . . At a bus stop . . . At half two in the morning.

Only my granny gets three!

L. xx

Okay. I really can't send that.

She deletes the mail.

Starts to type again.

Jim,

Great to meet you in the small hours and not quite get to talk.

Would love to . . .

(*To self.*) No.

Work manic busy right now.

Must sound busy and relaxed and all those other things the girls told me.

But be great to catch up sometime soon.

Hope all good with you.

Regards?

(*To self.*) Fuck sake.

It's going to have to be a smiley face.

There.

Except he needs my name.

(*Typing.*) Lucy.

Jim   'Lucy'.

Lucy   Smiley face.

(*To self.*) Send.

§

Jim   The email comes through with the name Lucy. I don't know a Lucy. It's just titled 'Hi'. Like a virus but I have to open it because.

. . .

At least she's got in touch. Surely she wouldn't get in touch if she wasn't interested?

She puts a smiley face. Oh.

I need to show some balls now. Got to recommend going somewhere. Got to get the date.

She says she's busy so maybe I should go for next week. Maybe I should play casual?

Tony says. 'If you can make any modern woman doubt herself in the slightest way then she will want you for ever.'

Tony is single.

I'm going to email her in two hours. On a lunch break.

That's what London urban professionals do, I think.

§

Lucy   First dates are magical.

There's absolutely no pressure to do anything. It's the opposite.

I know we don't have to kiss. I know I don't have to go back to his. We can leave with everything having gone well.

We will have flirted a little. Feel a little light-headed from a couple of drinks and the noise of the bar. Step out into the night air. Walk by the river.

And we can leave each other. We won't have argued. We won't have done anything silly.

We would have just been two people meeting.

It's as perfect as it gets.

But he's rung. And we're going out. We're going out on Thursday. At seven. He sounds so confident. Like he's done it a thousand times.

We're going for dinner.

He's nice.

He's not John though.

§

Jim *moves next to* **Lucy**. *They don't look at one another.*

Jim   She looks so relaxed and at ease. All the time. Like she's done it all a thousand times.

Her arms brushes against mine as we walk. Our fingers even bump into one another as she talks. I think about taking her hand. And don't.

She talks with such enthusiasm for everything. Without fear. The whole world is there to be attacked for her. Work. London. Life.

I'm running just to catch up with her.

I hope she doesn't see me sweating.

Lucy   And there are more dates.

In restaurants. In bars. On a boat. In an eye overlooking the city, with champagne and kissing.

And they are all exciting. And they are just like the first. But better.

Jim   I think about her every second of the day afterwards. Replay each moment of every date. Work. And the rest of living. Seems to have faded away in this haze of Lucy.

I can't dream for daydreaming about her.

I know that she isn't doing this. I know that she is still living her life.

Lucy   I'm in trouble now you see?

I'm better on my own.

That's what works for me. I'm not unhappy. I'm happy. Really.

§

So I go a little bit giddy these days at the thought of him. Hearing him. Seeing him. It's a sugar rush. First burst of spring, when you uncoil yourself from the utter misery of January and February and the sun bursts through. City parks filled with optimistic lunch-eaters. Drinks outside bars on streets. Walking on the canal to work even though it takes half an hour longer. And with hummingbirds in your belly and this odd sense of warmth that lifts your whole body.

He wears this jacket. All the time. With a wool lining. It cups his jaw, brushes his smile. His legs are so long. His walk.

The weight of his chest when he moves into me.

There's something in his eyes. He looks like he'll look after me. And I know that's not very New Age. I know I'm letting Germain down but I want to be looked after. And I want someone to look after too. What's wrong with that?

And what's wrong with wanting him to ring?

Every second of every day.

What's wrong with that?

I stayed at his for the first time. We just talked. There was never any sense of . . .

Talking all through the night.

He had put toothpaste on a new toothbrush for me when I went into the bathroom.

I think I'm supposed to feel owned or belittled or. But it just makes me melt.

She goes.

§

Jim *retreats to his space.*

He takes his clothes off. Down to his boxer shorts. He thinks about removing these.

He stops short.

He looks up, as if looking in a mirror.

He flinches a little at the sight of himself.

Jim   Fat fuck.

Skinny fuck.

Fucking fuck.

And she is coming to stay at mine. And this time there is a real sense that . . .

Lucy *is on her bed. She wears a dressing gown. She peers underneath her dressing gown.*

Lucy   In a book I'd be worried about whether or not my underwear was matching.

In a book I'd be worried about lighting.

The size of my arse.

My boobs.

. . .

Instead I look at my pale skin. The blotches on it look like splashes of acid. My eyes used to be a colour. Now red wire creeps all over them.

My hair creeps down from my head and wants to be all over my face.

She stands. Looks down at her legs.

My toes look crippled.

My thighs spill into one another in an undefined blotchy, gloopy mess. Wobble and wobble and.

My knees. A man's knees. My dad's knees.

He's supposed to remove my clothes and erupt in sexual arousal. Tearing more and more off until we lie breathless on the bed.

Will he know to be gentle with me?

Will he know to be a little rough with me?

§

We go for a walk.

Because I want to delay it all. The idea of someone else in my space. In my little room.

Jim   We walk for three hours in the park that night. And. I know. With her. It's where I want to stay. Just listening to her talk. About anything.

Every little sentence she shares with me about her past feels like a gift.

I start to think I should be kissing her. I wonder why I haven't done anything mad and romantic. Like pull her towards me and kiss her under the moon.

A better man would have kissed her by now.

Is she bored?

I don't want to appear like a fourteen-year-old walking cock who wants to jump on her in a ditch at first chance.

So I keep my distance a bit. Do lots of looking up to the stars as if I'm drinking this night in.

But I think I come across as a fourteen-year-old cock without the courage to jump on a girl in a ditch at first chance.

We sit at the base of a tree.

We're cold.

She asks me to put my arm around her.

Sit there for a while. In silence. I hear her breathing. It's so loud. And clear. And.

I lean into her. My face touches her cold cheek. Her eyes look up into mine and I fall into her pupils.

We kiss.

Her lips are warm. Her breath speeds up. My heart booms. The sound of her coat rustling as she grabs the back of my head. The denim of her jeans as she puts her leg over mine. Her hair falls across my cheek. I've never smelt anything like it.

We run back to her house.

We run.

This is as happy as I've ever been.

Let me stay right here I think.

§

(*Trying not to cry.*) Can we stop now?

I'd like to stop.

He creeps towards **Lucy***'s bedroom.*

She nervously removes her dressing gown. She is wearing her underwear.

Jim *steps into* **Lucy***'s bedroom.*

Their chests rise and fall. Hearts thump. Nerves. Fear. Excitement.

Lucy *holds out her hand.* **Jim** *moves towards her.*

Lights fall.

Lights rise.

Jim is lying on the bed. He holds **Lucy** *from behind. He smells her hair. He smiles.*

He shuts his eyes and opens them again.

Jim   I won't talk about it.

I won't say anything. Not to you. Or anyone else.

Because some things you can't. Some things you never should.

Except to say that it wasn't frightening. And I didn't feel like I'd disappointed her. Or that I was wrong or.

It was the only time anything ever felt natural with a girl in my life. And I didn't want to run away and hide afterwards. I didn't want to do anything.

Except stay there.

In her bed.

§

He closes his eyes. He takes his finger and traces the outline of **Lucy***'s body without touching her. He traces from her shoulder all the way down past her hip and thighs and knees and calves. He finally takes* **Lucy***'s hand. She sleepily responds by holding his hand into her body.*

He gently kisses her and moves off.

She rises, sleepily.

Lucy   I don't look at my body once.

He looks at it all the time. In a good way!

His eyes soften as they open up. He kisses me so gently. He holds me. Like I'm suspended in air. The sound of his breath is strong and safe. And after we . . .

And I'm lying there on my front.

He leans over me. This big powerful man. Hanging over me.

His hair tickles my back as he kisses my body.

It's magical.

Happy here.

Happy now.

§

She is lost in the thought for a moment. She composes herself again.

I feel like asking him to stay. To never leave this room. But I know that soon he will leave and . . .

I'm going to ring him that night. I'm not going to write anything down. I might not even say anything. Just listen to him breathe.

§

A clothed **Jim** *returns. He walks to the wall of* **Lucy***'s bedroom. He sees something. A photograph.*

Jim   I hate him. Whoever he is.

The one in the photographs. The one in most of the photographs. Look at all of them. He's good looking.

He's tanned in lots of the pictures.

He looks like a happy person.

A whole history on the wall. Friends, fun, happiness. A life.

Lucy *looks to* **Jim***. She looks to the My Little Pony on her bed.*

Lucy   He notices the My Little Pony on the bed. I spent all this time making him believe I was a woman with a career and now he sees I'm a thumb-sucking child with a doll with pink hair. Would have hid the thing if I knew that he was. Would have put different sheets on the bed. Would've.

I wonder what he's thinking when his eyes scan the room. He probably wanted a woman and he's ended up with Glasgow's own Little Mermaid.

Jim *walks around the bedroom.*

Jim   Cotton buds tied to the door handle. A picture of a geisha girl on the wall. Flowers on the cupboard drawers.

White and green. White lamps. White sheets. Her suit jacket hung on the wall.

A weird pony with pink hair.

Makes me want to hold her.

All of it makes me want to hold her.

He kisses **Lucy** *as he goes to leave her room.*

Jim   Yeah. I know what that is before you start . . .

He returns to his space.

Men all want a woman with vulnerability, don't they? We all want a little girl we can protect from the wind. But that's not it. Not it at all.

Just nice to know that someone else gets scared of things.

Does that make sense?

Your face makes me want to scream.

I'm not a bad person.

I'm not.

§

Jim   Hello.

Lucy *laughs.*

Jim   Hi.

Lucy *listens to her phone.*

Jim (*smiles*)   Hello.

What you doing?

Lucy   . . . Nothing.

They listen to one another breathe down the phone. Some giggling.

Jim   You should go to sleep.

Lucy   So should you.

Jim   Leave the phone by your pillow.

Lucy   Kiss me down the phone.

Jim   You what?

Lucy   Kiss me down the phone.

Jim *does it.*

Lucy   I'll dream of you.

§

Jim *arrives with a bunch of flowers. He drops them by* **Lucy**'s *bed. He smiles.*

She looks at him. They leap into bed together. They disappear under the covers, frantic movement beneath the duvet, breathless, giggling.

A still breathless **Lucy** *emerges from the duvet at the bottom of the bed and slides out. She laughs.*

§

An arm appears from under the bottom of the duvet cover. **Lucy** *is hauled back under the covers. She shrieks with laughter.*

§

Jim *starts to do some press-ups. This lasts a while.*

Jim   Dinner tonight. I'm an actual grown-up. Taking a woman. For a meal.

Where should I take her? Need to get that sort of thing right. Need to know where to go in the city.

He starts to do some sit-ups.

We're stepping out together! Man and woman. Dinner.

He looks at himself in a mirror. He looks at his stomach in profile. Tries to make it look flatter.

Lucy *enters spraying perfume. The back of her dress is open.*

She stops and looks at **Jim**. *He looks at her. She looks beautiful. His face lets her know.*

She turns to him and points to the back of her undone dress.

He zips her up. She dashes off.

The smell of **Lucy**'s *perfume hits* **Jim**. *He falls back on the bed in a blissful haze.*

§

Jim   And we go for breakfast. A lot.

And I take her everywhere that I've had a dream of being with someone.

Beaches, clifftops, piers, parks . . . I've walked them all on my own. And now I'm with her.

I pounce on her in every spot. Jumping into ditches at first chance!

He closes his eyes. A sigh of pleasure.

It's much better than any of my dreams.

Lucy *puts some music on.* **Jim** *knows every lyric. He throws* **Lucy** *on the bed. He stands on the bed and sings the song to her.*

He leaps on top of her. They erupt in a fit of giggles.

§

Lucy   And he moves in.

Jim *hurries off. He returns with a full suitcase.*

Lucy   And it all feels complete.

Jim *puts his suitcase down by the side of the bed.*

Lucy   We're as one.

She moves to **Jim**. *She hands him a key.*

They hold one another.

Blackout.

Act Two

Lights rise . . .

Jim   I used to have a drawer in her cupboard. And I loved my drawer. Now we have sides of the bed.

Jim *moves to his side of the bed. Proud. He puts on some music. 'No Name' by Ryan O'Shaughnessy plays.*

Lucy   There's a man in my flat. My man.

Jim   And I start to feel like it's my home too. Our flat.

Lucy   And we start to feel like we work as a team.

Jim   That feeling of coming home to someone. I know what you're thinking. I know that's supposed to be sexist or old-fashioned or.

But that feeling of having her come home to me to is just . . .

§

Lucy *comes in with her bag, as if straight from work.* **Jim** *lifts her in his arms and throws her on to the bed. He jumps on her like a teenager in a ditch.*

She lifts her head.

Lucy   'Imagine the tiniest thing that annoys you about your partner. Then times that by about a thousand.' That's what Kim said when I told her he was moving in. But it's nonsense. He performs all these tiny acts of kindness that swell my heart.

He runs me a bath when I tell him I'm coming home from the station. He cooks. He pours me a glass of wine as I'm getting changed and he makes dinner. Pulls out my chair as we sit to eat.

Jim   We make something together. We make a home. With candles. And lots of cotton buds. And we tend to that home. We cook. We clean. We repair it. Care for it.

Lucy *lies on the floor. She is watching TV.* **Jim** *takes a pillow and puts it under her head.*

He lies with his head on her stomach.

She strokes his head.

Jim   Lying on the floor watching a DVD with this woman is the greatest thing in the world.

§

We have great long talks over breakfasts. In market places. Croissants in French patisseries, muffins in Smithfield Market and yogurt and honey on the street at the Greek. On heaths, at lidos and gardens and museums and.

We are part of the city. We.

Lucy   It's not just the knowing of him. It's knowing every tiny dream he ever had. All the ones that never came true and the ones that still might.

§

Jim   And people like me better when I'm with her. They smile at us as we walk down the canal holding hands. They must know.

Lucy   He talks to strangers. All the time. Helps women with over-sized suitcases up mountainous stairs. Plays with kids running into our legs at restaurants. And he's wonderful with all of them. People like him before he even opens his mouth.

Jim   Take her to the zoo and fall asleep on our tiny patch of grass in Regent's Park. Steal a kiss in the aquarium by the penguins. Chase her down halls of the Portrait Gallery.

We drink warm wine on Parliament Hill on a tartan woolly rug. And when it gets cold I wrap it around her shoulders and pull her into me.

Lucy   And he takes me to the Roebuck on Richmond Hill.

Jim   We drink wine and look out on to the lights of the city. What a view. I like it there better than Parliament Hill I think. And I know that's not cool to say but.

'Richmond'.

It's important to aspire to something.

§

Lucy   My mum meets him and tells me that I will marry him.

My dad says it's the first boyfriend I've ever had who he hasn't wanted to throw out of the front door.

Jim   I'm so proud to walk next to her.

I'd like to tell her that but it feels like my throat has turned to steel every time I try and say anything with any true meaning.

So I do other stuff. I sing. A lot. And dance. A bit like my dad, which is disconcerting but makes her laugh, guaranteed.

§

He starts to undress during the following.

And other stuff like coming into the room naked. Pretending I've forgotten something. And then leaving again.

He leaves. He returns, naked. Does exactly as he's described. Leaves again.

And of course there's the willy dance. She loves the willy dance.

We see his back as he starts to bounce up and down in front of **Lucy**.

Lucy (*laughing*)   Oh my God! What's it doing? It's going round in a circle!

Jim *is now performing star jumps, knee-raises, etc.* **Lucy** *laughs herself into the floor. He leaves.*

Lucy *recovers her breath.*

§

Lucy I tell him that I love him. And I know how much of me is in those tiny words. Ones I've never meant before.

I thought I did. But this is different. This is.

Jim I wake up with her and want to open the windows and scream to the city that she is with me. And I am with her. She has all of me.

I wonder if she knows.

§

Lucy I hear things all the time in the flat. I wake up scared and I don't want to move. It's the noises in the city.

He gets up naked, goes and checks all the rooms and comes back to tell me no one's there.

I start to clean a lot. And cook things like muffins and cookies. I don't cook.

Mum says I'm nesting but I tell her to fuck off.

But really I do think about it. I imagine what our kids would look like. I smile to myself on the tube when I think of baby names.

'Francesca'. 'Miles'.

Not very Glasgow I know. But.

What's happening to me?

§

Jim Nothing ever stands still in the city. And if you do then you get left behind. I have a credit card to improve my credit rating. I buy a dreadful car on HP to do the same thing.

A Honda Civic. It even sounds . . .

Because otherwise I'm going to be fifty-five and without a mortgage.

And if I'm going to be a real man. For her.

She talks about a new home all the time.

About trellises and ponds and decking and . . .

So I work harder. And harder.

I put in the hours of the ultimate urban professional. I arrive and leave with the cleaners and kiss my love when I flop into the bed at home.

I know they're watching me. I'm at that age when I either step up. Or I stay where I am until I move to Swindon.

I've started to like going into work. I like to be among the crowd of high achievers on the Waterloo & City Line with their iPads and purposeful walks. I get competitive about ties and the appearance of shoes. I wear my smartest overcoat and always tip the busker playing 'Redemption Song'. Very badly. I stand up a little bit taller.

Cos she's with me now. In everything I do. I feel like anything is possible with her at my side. Nothing left to be frightened of.

I will tear down the walls for her.

§

Sundays are when you leave the city. It all stops. Step out to the suburbs.

To see her parents.

Her mother seems so pleased to see her. I wish my mum looked at me like that. But of course she does! She's Lucy! Imagine if this girl was your daughter. Your chest would be crushed with pride.

I'm left in the living room with her father. I couldn't think of anything worse, to be honest.

I don't like his voice. Or his house. Or the way he potters around his garage doing nothing at all. And that newspaper he buys. One step away from a flick-read of *Mein Kampf*.

Probably sings 'Land of Hope snd Glory' in his striped pyjamas and moccasins. Salutes the red arrows of a morning.

And his full head of hair. And his overly firm handshake. And those bloody pink golf jumpers and boating shoes.

But.

But.

Lucy   I watch them walking in the garden together as my dad shows him the garage. My mum points out that they have the same walk. And she raises her eyebrow. And I want to punch her at this point but I'm embarrassed to admit that a little bit of me loves it.

I love my dad. Not cool. But I just do.

Jim   I can see his nerves when he starts conversation after conversation that both of us try to keep afloat. He offers me whisky. And I know he doesn't drink whisky. But that's what men are supposed to do when they're on their own and can't think of a word to say. And he's trying to make me welcome.

He's so kind. His voice comes right from the base of his belly. Booms with warmth for me.

He tells me that he has never seen his daughter as happy as she is now.

I think this is the most generous thing anyone has ever said to me.

If Lucy were my daughter I wouldn't be capable of anything other than the threat of committed violence to anyone who wanted to go near her.

I hope that one day I can offer a lost idiot some whisky. From my spirits chest. And make him feel loved and accepted within five minutes. In my study. In my home. In the suburbs.

Gordon is a real man.

Even with a name like that. And a jumper like that.

Gordon is a real man.

Lucy   He sits at the table. Next to my brother. And my mother. And it all looks right.

He compliments my mum on the food. He insists on washing up. And making everyone tea when we finish.

He asks my brother if he can play Grand Theft Auto V with him. And my brother tries to look annoyed and embarrassed.

But all he does is look like the coolest man in the world has asked to be his best mate.

Jim   I like being there. With them. And listening to their stories of Lucy when she wore NHS glasses and odd luminous socks. And wore tie-dye T-shirts and kissed a poster of Damon Albarn every morning.

Lucy actually goes red at their stories and bemoans the fact that her dad constantly embarrasses her. She can't see that they're all telling her how much they love her.

Lucy   I sometimes don't want to leave the house at night. But we do.

Jim   I don't want to leave Gordon and Anne's house. It was like being cuddled for three hours.

Gordon shakes my hand as we leave. And puts the other hand on my shoulder. And tells me to make sure Lucy 'behaves'. I want to be like Gordon. With his wife. And his children. And his home. And his garage.

I don't even want to let go of his hand.

Lucy   Both back to work tomorrow. Back to the city.

Jim   So we go home. To our home.

§

Jim *starts to polish his shoes.*

Lucy   He has an interview for a promotion at work. He tells me he's nervous.

Jim It means a possible partnership. It means a company car. It means shares. Alright, so I too am now going to do a job which means making money for people who already have lots of money but I am feeling brilliant about it.

It means I can realistically live! Like a man! A city man!

I read books on body language for my interview. I rehearse my presentation in front of the mirror and record it with a Dictaphone.

Lucy I catch him doing this. It's beautiful.

Jim I practise 'the voice of authority', 'the voice of confidence'.

Lucy Tells me he's terrified. He never told me anything like that before.

Jim I picture an office. I picture a Labrador. And a conservatory. And a shed with a telly.

Lucy Makes me adore him.

§

Jim *starts to comb his hair. He comes in to* **Lucy** *and holds out his arms as if to ask 'What do you think?'*

Lucy You look amazing.

Jim Really?

Lucy I'd do yer.

Jim Would you promote me too?

Lucy There's a huge list of things I'd do to you.

Jim It's alright?

Lucy You look so handsome.

She starts to do **Jim**'s *tie.*

Jim Thank you. Not too Channel 4 News? (*The tie.*)

Lucy Not at all.

Jim   I'm. I'm. Thank you, you know? Thank you.

Lucy   I'm so proud of you. Good luck, my love.

Jim *kisses* **Lucy**.

Lucy *has gone.*

Jim (*to self*)   I love you. With every bit of me.

I want to spend all of my life with this woman.

§

He starts to brush his teeth.

I want to take her on a holiday where I don't lose days looking for the cheapest flight I can get. Or make sandwiches for the car so we don't have to pay for stuff at the airport.

Lucy   Kim says holidays are for proposals.

Jim   Or start counting out euros to check whether I can enter a restaurant or not. Because it's what this woman deserves. You know?

Lucy   And I laugh it off.

And then I can't stop picturing it. And it makes me almost explode with excitement.

Jim   A real man would sweep her away and leave her with a tumbling tummy and tingly toes . . . instead of taking her on Monarch Airlines.

He spits and leaves. Determined. Sharp.

§

We wait to go in. There are four of us. Immersed in mobile phones and feigning the relaxed aura of confident men.

My suit is seven years old and I used to carry a lot more timber. The others have hair products. And shiny shoes with buckles. And expensive suitcases.

Their ties are things of exquisite beauty.

I talk to one of them. I shouldn't have. His voice sounds like a brilliant education and a school with lots of playing fields. He smiles, looks totally at ease, as if he belongs. And I just . . .

A light shines brightly on him. Brighter and brighter. He shifts a little. Hot, uncomfortable. Blinks into the bright light. He looks as if he will shrink into the ground.

§

Lucy   He texts.

The light fades down. **Jim***'s head falls.*

Lucy   I wish he'd rung.

Jim   I wore the wrong shoes.

Lucy   I hate to think of him walking to the station on his own. And feeling . . .

I wish he'd rung. I would have gone to meet him. Took him out.

Held him.

Jim *slopes back into the room. He takes his tie off and slumps on to the bed.*

§

Lucy   I suggest a holiday.

He's worked so hard. And he deserves it. We deserve it.

Jim   I failed her.

Lucy   I want to pay for it, you see. He looks like he'll cry at the suggestion. I don't care about money. I don't need money. We have a roof. We have a bed. We have each other.

Jim   Failed her when I should have made her proud.

Lucy   I don't want a yacht. If you've got a yacht then chances are you're a total fucking knob.

Jim   How can I offer a life for her? How can I suggest a marriage? A family?

And a house with a garage.

And now's the time you see. We're not twenty-something any more. Nothing is casual. There are expectations.

§

Jim   People have stopped going out in the city. They go to restaurants and leave early. They discuss floor lighting and marble sideboards. And weekends to the country.

She waits for me to take a step forward into manhood.

To be like the others with the cycling obsession and the skiing holidays and the fucking bonus.

A real man earns more than twenty-four grand a year.

A real man.

Lucy *gets into bed.*

§

Lucy   He constantly punishes himself for all the things he doesn't have.

I want to scream at him 'You have me!' 'You have me!'

Jim *turns away from* **Lucy** *and falls asleep.*

Lucy   And he won't talk now. Looks like he's falling down a hole.

She climbs out of bed.

§

He carries a look of disappointment which hangs in the air like a sad song. So I try and talk to him.

Jim *starts to try and undress* **Lucy**. *She does her best to wrestle away from him, slightly annoyed. He persists. And persists.*

Lucy   He always says there's nothing wrong. Which drives me insane. And he always wants to move on. Forget about it.

Jim *is trying to kiss and fondle* **Lucy**. *She remains entirely impassive.*

Lucy   His way of doing this is to try and sleep with me.

She pushes him away. **Jim** *walks away, disgruntled.*

§

Jim   She starts to pay for things. Dinner. Shopping. Train tickets. She does it nonchalantly to protect my pride but it feels like I'm being drawn and quartered.

I'm warned at work for my 'poor time-keeping and hostile attitude'. Hostile?

Lucy   And I know that I should love him through everything but his self-loathing eats at me. I want to be supportive. It's wearing me down. Money is nothing. Money is a nonsense.

It must be something else. He doesn't look at me the same way. He sometimes doesn't look at me at all. He used to eat me up with his eyes and it made me feel . . .

And now I just feel alone.

Jim *returns. He sits on the edge of the bed.* **Lucy** *is sitting on the bed behind him.*

He puts on 'No Name'. He turns to **Lucy** *after a while. She turns off the music and leaves.*

Jim   I try and mend things. I always try and mend things. Put us back to where we were. When I wanted time to freeze.

I want to kiss her at the base of the tree.

§

When I come home to her she says nothing. Sometimes she's already in bed.

When she comes home to me we say nothing. Sometimes I'm already fed.

He climbs into bed. **Lucy** *comes in with her bag as if straight from work. She wearily climbs into bed. They lie next to one another with their eyes open. Each one waiting for the other to act.* **Lucy** *gives up. She rolls over and goes to sleep.*

Jim   They say it's 'only one less worry' but its bollocks. It's everything in the city decides where you go. And who with. And where you're definitely never going to go.

Lucy   I stick with this. Because I love him. And I get scared too.

I wait for him. However long. I want this man to be my husband.

§

But right now I can't stand the sight of these walls. Our walls.

I have to get out.

She leaves.

§

Jim *tosses and turns in bed.*

He sits up, frustrated. He looks at the clock. He checks his phone. Nothing.

Jim   Slow. Fucking. Torture. Gets to ten and I just want a text to say that she's okay. Nothing comes. Gets to eleven. She's leaving now. Tell me you're leaving. Eleven thirty. On a train now. Tell me you're coming home. Tell me you're coming home.

It's half past midnight. Must have gone on. Why hasn't she sent me a message? Must just be in a late bar. In a club. Said she wasn't but we all have changes of plans.

Half past one. Where is she? I have to ring now. I have to be the possessive fool. I'll just ring to check she's alright but I'm still the possessive one.

He holds the phone in his hand.

I want to be cool. I want to be cool and unruffled. And give her a sleepy kiss when she gets in. And not ask where she's been. Or who with.

He dials her number.

Phone off.

Who's she with? Who's she with? Who's she with?

Half past two.

Half past three.

Four o'clock.

Jim *flings himself under the duvet just as* **Lucy** *staggers in drunk and almost falls into the bed.*

Lucy   I love you.

Jim *pretends to be asleep.*

§

Jim   Nothing and no one stands still in the city. You must be planning something or you've ceased to be. There is no present here.

Will I marry her? Have children with her?

When? When?

He takes a lamp and puts it on a table next to the bed. He adjusts the position of the lamp until he is satisfied.

Lucy *watches on, a little bemused.*

Jim *climbs into her bed.*

They pick out a book each. They climb into bed in synch.

They turn on their lamps in synch.

They open their books and begin to read.

Lucy   My heart has stopped thumping.

Jim *is getting dressed for work through the following . . .*

§

Lucy   He's stopped taking a shower in the morning. Walks out to work without looking in the mirror.

Stopped brushing his teeth.

Jim *looks down at his stomach. He folds his body in half so his stomach spills over his trousers even more.*

Lucy   He drinks. Incessantly. His stomach has started to spill over the button of his trousers.

He's losing his hair.

Jim *pats his hair down.*

Jim   I work from home more and more. The days seem to mould into one another and I'm not making progress. There's nothing to look forward to now.

He picks up his work bag and leaves.

§

Lucy   We go for dinner and he spends the whole time watching other people. My stories aren't interesting any more.

Lucy *and* **Jim** *operate in their own spaces. They are as far from one another as they can be.*

Jim   I'm playing on consoles again.

I watch sport on the TV and shout about things that will never change my life or even alter it in the slightest.

Lucy   He used to iron his shirt for dinner with me. He polished his shoes once. Did fifty press-ups and all these sit-ups as if it would work half an hour before we went out. But I loved it.

Jim   She thinks a baby might change this. She thinks we're ready for the next stage.

I can't bring up a child. I've had the same toothbrush for over a year.

Lucy   We're stuck at a stage. We live only for ourselves. And only occasionally for each other.

I say I'm going to take my coil out and try for a baby.

§

Lucy *moves to* **Jim***. She touches him. He almost flinches.*

Jim   A baby?

Lucy   I tell him it takes couples our age an average of eighteen months to get pregnant. And then there's nine months more.

Jim   So, like. Two years? Two and a half?

Lucy *kisses* **Jim***. It's odd. Awkward. Stiff.*

He tries to respond. They undress as little as possible in order to have sex. Socks still on, etc. It looks what it is, perfunctory.

They have sex in silence. They don't look at one another.

He rolls off her and stands away from the bed.

Lucy *lifts up her legs with her hands. She looks like an upturned crab. She stays in this position. She checks her watch.* **Jim** *looks at her. Horrified.*

Lucy   I read a piece in *Cosmo* that said it helps with the . . .

Jim *walks off.*

§

Jim *returns as* **Lucy** *disappears beneath the covers.*

Jim   Months come and go. And each time she emerges from the bathroom with that empty look I feel nothing but relief.

I fold her in my arms but she can't see that look on my face.

Lucy   What's the point of being with someone?

What's the point of companionship?

Why are we here? What are we making? What are we doing?

Jim *hugs* **Lucy**.

She withdraws from him.

§

Lucy   Richard from work takes me out for a drink. I haven't been out with the work lot for. Been not drinking. Not smoking. Not living for the hope of making a life.

He brings his brother called Jake. And he's everything you imagine someone called 'Jake' to be. Young. Firm-bodied. Cheeky. Untroubled. Fun.

Jim   I've stopped talking to anyone. Even Tony. I go and stay a night with him and I can't wait to run out of the door of the house he's bought. He looks brainwashed.

Lucy   It's turned him from a baby into a man.

Jim   He's married and has a child. Talks to me about responsibility. Talks to me about the power of two.

Lucy   Everyone has babies. Stopped going out.

Jim   There are no breakfasts alone.

Lucy   They live their lives like glossy Sunday supplements. Brown Labradors. Freshly grassed lawns. Rick Stein recipes and holidays in Fuji.

I don't want that bollocks. That's city bullshit. But I want a child. I want a life growing inside me. So much.

Jim   There are no more breakfasts alone.

Just brunches. With couples. Who spread broadsheet newspapers across large wooden tables in gastropubs. One of whom is incapable of talking of anything other than the excrement of her six-month-old. And the other complains that he hates his job. In the City. With his enormous bonus. And his wind-surfing in Fuji and his bloody five-thousand-pound push bike. And his 'PB' on Sunday up Box Hill.

They are moving to a four-bed. In Henley. How hateful his life must be.

Lucy   Every one of our friends merely reflects that fact that we are still. Stagnant.

Jim   He tells me how envious of me he is. That I get to do
something I 'love'.

I don't love it. It's all I can do. I'm a 'graphic designer'! I
want to say. I am still doing 'drawings' and I can go to work
in my pyjamas without anyone giving a shit. I make no money
for people with very little money and I have fuck-all money
myself! I have made no progress since my mum packed my
lunch.

I'm barely qualified to be a paper boy.

And you. You! Are not Bradley Wiggins. You're a mal-co-
ordinated middle-aged man from Putney. With a fat arse.

Lucy   And Jim is awful with them now. He just wants us all
to drink. And sulks when we don't.

Jim   Envious of me?

He shakes his head.

Lucy   We stop going out.

§

*They get out laptops. Sit on the bed as if watching TV. They do not look
at one another. This looks entirely routine.*

Lucy   So now we're in.

Jim   Watching television with our laptops in our laps.

Lucy   Will we be fifty years old and forget what one
another's lips taste like?

She slowly slaps her laptop shut and lies down.

Jim *slaps his laptop. He looks at* **Lucy***. He stands and moves away
from her as if nervous that she may hear the following.*

§

Jim   I can't look into those eyes any more.

I can't even kiss her any more.

The idea of.

I want the lights out now.

If she knew.

I don't feel excited about any part of it. Her skin. Her touch. Makes me feel dead.

I picture someone else when I'm.

Just to get aroused.

Because my body is that dead now.

The minute we finish I can't get far enough away. I know I have to look at her now. Can't just roll off into the bathroom.

But I'm not having that 'talk'.

I look at her.

She can see right through me.

She can see all the lies.

I'm hurting the only person who ever said they loved me.

And meant it.

§

Lucy *moves towards* **Jim**. *She is looking into his eyes. Close. He is somehow not looking at her.*

Lucy   He hates me. He is repulsed by me.

She tries to take **Jim**'s *hand. He is lifeless.*

Lucy   And I want so badly for him to put his arms around me and tell me everything's alright.

She reluctantly lets go of **Jim**'s *hand. Heartbroken.*

Lucy   I wonder if she's prettier than me. I wonder if she's funnier than me. Cleverer than me.

I wonder if he tells her little things about himself and if she feels like they belong to her.

I offered him all of me and it isn't good enough.

He used to look at me as if light beamed from my soul.

Now he just recoils when I try to touch him.

She tries to kiss **Jim**. *He remains stiff and lifeless.*

Lucy   And it breaks my darkened soul in two.

She looks devastated.

I want so badly for him to kiss me. And mean it.

§

Jim   I sleep with another girl that night. I sleep with Kim.

The betrayal was there the first text I sent her.

I tell her I'm in her area.

Which is the first lie.

From the minute we meet I can tell she is dressed up. For me. She looks right into my eyes. And then just below. And then into my eyes.

I'm flattered and excited.

I'd like to tell you that I don't think of Lucy during any of it. That I drank too much and one thing led to another and things just happened. But they don't. And they didn't.

The decision to kiss her takes over an hour. The thought begins when we're sat at the bar. She rests her hand on my thigh as she laughs. I think of kissing her. I think of Lucy.

Lucy *sits alone on the bed. She checks her watch.*

Jim   She likes my stories. Laughs at them. And it feels so good.

Lucy *tries to distract herself. She puts some music on.*

Jim   And neither of us want the night to end.

So we go on. We ignore the bouncers itching for an excuse to fight in the nightclub with no sign on the door. And the bar staff who hate you on sight. And the DJ posing as a cool bloke but in reality is a sex pest in his mid-thirties who lives with his mum.

The sex pest is playing PM Dawn. 'How have people become nostalgic for shit?' she says.

I smile and nod as if she's said the most funny and profound thing all at once. I'm already looking at her and wondering what her breasts look like without the clothes covering them.

And talking to her is so easy. It always is when you don't care.

She takes my hand when the lights come up and the club spills out. And we say nothing the entire way home. Perhaps if we stay silent then it will be like we've done nothing wrong.

I think of Lucy all the way to her flat in that taxi. I think of her waiting for me. And I try to get angry at her to justify . . .

I have sex with her. I have sex with Kim.

Drunk and floppy. And messy. And fumbling. And inadequate. And cold.

And in the morning. I leave. Without saying a word.

He begins to rip the sheets off the bed in disgust during the following.

And I feel like an animal.

I've hurt the one person who I loved completely.

Why do I hate her for loving me back?

Animal. Animal. Animal.

§

Lucy *(types)*   I never want to see or speak to you again.

Jim *reads the message on his laptop. He stands. He falls to the ground. He weeps a little. He thinks about typing. He shuts down his laptop.*

Lucy *starts to rip at her bedding. Hurling covers, etc. to the floor.*

She picks up her My Little Pony and starts to rip at it.

She tears down the pictures from the wall.

Blackout.

Act Three

Jim *is in his space. He sits on the floor. A pile of unopened mail scattered around him.*

Lucy *sits in a chair, addressing someone.*

Lucy   I should be married.

Jim   Should have a wife.

Lucy   See the next ten years stretching out in even colours.

Jim   But . . .

Lucy   But . . .

Jim   But . . .

Lucy   But . . .

Jim   I can't see anything.

Lucy   Except . . .

Jim   A pile of unopened letters on my front doormat.

Lucy *begins to move around the room.*

Lucy   His clothes still under the bed.

Jim   Her face in my head.

Lucy   His coat on a hook by the door.

Jim   Bin over spilling onto the floor.

Lucy   His toothbrush in a glass on the sink.

Jim   I used to hear her sing from beyond the shower door. Laugh down the phone to her mum.

But now nothing and no one.

Lucy   No one.

Jim   No more Gumtree mates. I can't talk about mushrooms at 3 a.m. on a damp sofa in Dalston.

So I'm in my bedsit. The ultimate failure of living.

Lucy *retreats to her bed. She puts on her dressing gown.*

§

Lucy   I can't set foot outside the door. I don't want to *emerge* anywhere.

Jim   Every day reaches out like an eternity.

Lucy   And every meeting is exposing. An opportunity for humiliation.

Jim   All I can hear are the muffled voices from above, the stomping feet and raised voices. I hear people all day. Never more than ten feet away from other people. Frustrated people. Angry people.

Lucy   It occurred to me that each time I flush the toilet hundreds of people are doing the same thing at the same time all within a mile radius of me. People. Everywhere.

Jim   I loved you.

Lucy   I love you.

Jim   Can I just . . .

Can I take a minute. Because . . .

Lucy   I can't ring my mum. Can't ring my brother. Can't ring anyone.

Cos it wasn't just me preparing for a life with you. It was them too.

Jim   I still haven't told my sister. How can I tell her what I've done?

Lucy   I can't tell them.

§

Jim   I go out. A lot. Drink in bars with brown leather sofas and gold taps.

Slump at my stool until I feel the lights come up.

Lucy   I retreat.

Jim   You used to stand beside me.

Lucy   My friends don't want to hear my sad stories.

Jim   I thought the nausea would go after this long. The gut-wrenching disgust with what I . . .

Lucy   They talk about pregnancies and holidays and house improvements. I am sitting on the bed my mum bought for me drenching tissues with bits of pain.

§

Jim   I'm warned at work. Officially now. And very little is official where I work. They even wear ties. With a witness in a cold grey room with lots of stern expressions. I can see in their eyes that they've let me go already.

Lucy   I don't want to hear it.

I can't hear the words he's going to say.

Jim   But I can't not hear her voice. I ring all the time. Until she begs me not to and begins to cry.

I can't stand the sound of her crying.

Lucy *sits on the bed. She has the phone to her ear. She drops the phone and begins to cry.*

§

Lucy   Every tiny piece of me I opened up to you.

Even think about getting undressed in front of you and I want to throw up.

I hate the idea that you've seen my naked skin. I hate the fact that you know things about me that no one else ever has or ever . . .

§

Jim   I walk across Waterloo Bridge and stare into the river below. It churns and swells, erupts and subsides. It's a dirty brown, green spew.

Lucy *is getting ready to go out over the following.*

Lucy   I'm so angry with him. Make a decision to fight back. Go out. In the city.

Jim   A woman who sounds Romanian tries to charge me ten pounds for a picture with a chameleon. She pulls at my coat as I walk away from her.

Lucy   I ring Katie. Tell her I haven't seen her for ages. Tell her it'd be great to 'have a big girls' night'. She knows I don't mean it but she is on her own.

Jim   A bearded man with black hands and a yellow neck asks me if I can spare any change. When I say no he looks like he wants to kill me.

Lucy   We run out of things to say to each other within two drinks. So we do shots. Make a show of trying to laugh a lot as if we are having the time of our lives.

Jim   A man in a purple bib thrusts a free paper into my stomach and a woman kicks my heel and swears at me as she marches through the station.

Lucy   All the while trying to scout the room to see if any men are watching us.

They aren't. Not the nice men.

Just the rapey-looking ones.

In lacquered shoes with buckles. And shirt buttons done up to their windpipes. And hair gel . . .

One asks me if I want a drink. He calls me 'babes'. I want to bite his nose off. But I say yes.

Jim *opens his laptop. He begins to type . . .*

Lucy   Drink so much that I am anaesthetised.

Jim   I wonder where you are. I picture you in the city. Are you lost like me?

Lucy   We go on. Make a move to go to the cab and he pulls me against a wall and starts to kiss me. Rams his hand up my leg. He's trying to grab my . . . in the middle of The Strand.

It takes everything to push him away. Off me.

I start to run towards the bus stop. Katie calls after me. He calls me a cunt. That word is just . . . And then he laughs. And shouts that I am a cock-tease.

The pavement wobbles and comes up to grab me and my knee cracks against something hard.

I wake up with my eyes half shut by mascara in my drink-sodden clothes.

Jim   I get why you don't want to see me. I just don't know how you do it so easily.

Lucy   Every time you sleep with someone they take a piece of your soul. I don't think I have anything left now. For anyone.

Jim   How you can just shut a door?

§

Lucy   I'm sick all the time. I just want someone to put their arms around me and tell me everything's alright.

Jim   I managed to go to work for a few days.

They look at you at first and they don't register. But then they look into your eyes. There's a flash of fear on their faces. They take a step back from you.

Its no one else's problem, is it?

Lucy   I was supposed to be a senior buyer by now. Instead I'm hiding in a bedroom and inventing stomach trouble and 'women's problems'.

Women's problems make you redundant in this city.

Jim   I look at people doing their everyday things. Shopping.
Drinking coffee. Smoking. Playing with their iPhones. They
look like nothing matters. Like they have all the time in the
world. Like today is just another day.

I'd do anything to feel like that.

Lucy   Except now my women's problems become real ones.

There is a baby growing inside of me.

She tosses and turns in her bed.

§

Jim   I wish I didn't dream about you. But I do. It's beautiful.
We're walking through the park at night. You tear your
T-shirt off and run through the trees screaming like a lunatic.
I chase after you. We have sex at the bottom of a willow tree.

We lie on the grass and listen to the leaves in the wind. And
talk about everything and a lot of nothing.

§

Lucy   It's five weeks old.

This 'thing'.

Jim   I'd like to tell you that I was complacent. Because that's
just human nature. And we all.

I'd like to tell you something.

Other than I regret it with every.

And I never stopped knowing how special you are.

I'm sorry. I'm sorry.

Can we? Can we? I don't know if I can carry on.

Sorry.

Lucy It is a thing. The nurse is careful not to give it any qualification. And it has to be a thing I think. To me. Now it does. Because . . .

I have everything that I ever wanted. Except you've gone away.

Jim I know I'm not supposed to tell you any of this.

Tony said I should act aloof and entirely over the whole fucking thing. And then you'd come running back. He said women only come back when they're entirely sure you're over it.

So this is my go at aloof.

I'm not so good at it.

It's because my soul has been scooped out since you've left.

I know I'm not supposed to talk about this stuff.

But you're the only one I talk to.

Hope you're well.

But sort of hope you're suffering too.

Really suffering.

You have me. xxx

§

Lucy Jim,

You're right. You shouldn't be telling me any of this. You can pass it off as being sensitive but you're being a bully.

You are playing the 'woe is me' and hoping I run to you all concerned and make everything alright.

You're a bully.

Yes. I love you. Yes, I'm sad that we're not together. But no. I'm so determined not to let this ruin my life. I'm not your carer.

I know how cruel that looks written down but you're not being fair to me.

Ask yourself why we're not together.

Sorry this seems so cruel. But don't you dare use the word heartless.

You stopped looking at me.

You made me hate myself.

You made me think I was nothing.

I don't want to feel like that any more.

I do love you.

I wish I didn't love you.

Please don't email me.

If you email again I won't read it.

You had my heart. You still do. You're just not allowed to play with it anymore.

I hope that you are happier soon.

L.

§

Jim *lies on the ground. He closes his eyes. He takes his finger and traces the outline of what he imagines is* **Lucy***'s body, without touching her. He traces from her shoulder all the way down past her hip and thighs and knees and calves.*

§

Jim *reaches out to take* **Lucy***'s hand. He grasps at thin air. He opens his eyes. He looks as if he is going to break.*

Jim   I know you said not to email you.

But you said not to phone you.

Or text you.

Or write to you.

But you haunt me.

You sign off to me now with nothing. Not even love or a kiss or . . . you probably give your clients more. When did I start meaning so little to you?

You have me. xx

§

Lucy   I haven't held down food for a long time. I feel like I will break in the middle of Victoria Station. The coldness of strangers makes me weep out loud.

They barge and tut and spin me round. And when I fall to the ground and start to weep they retreat as if I'm another nutter dribbling on the platform.

People here are cruel, violent and brutal. And they do it all without saying a word.

I can't take another step forward. Frozen to Platform Four.

Jim   I'd like to tell you something.

Other than I'm scared. Other than I'm terrified.

Other than I'm a weak. Weak . . .

Lucy   I don't understand why I work. I don't understand what life is for. I don't understand why anyone thinks that love is anything other than death.

Solitary is the only thing that makes sense these days. Especially in the city. How else do you . . . ?

Can we stop now?

I'd like to stop.

§

Jim   I go to clubs and look at women I'd never have the courage to talk to.

But now I drink enough to talk to them. I talk about you. I tell them that you are my world. They move away from me as though I were another nutter screaming at the London sky.

Lucy   I let the phone ring out now. How can I tell anyone that I've failed? And it's not long before people just stop ringing in the city. Two calls. Three.

Because people just move on, you see.

And you're forgotten.

There's always someone new in the city. Always something new.

Jim   I went a whole day where the only person who spoke to me was someone who asked me if I'd like a club card.

Lucy   And so I'm cut off and cast aside within a matter of weeks. Facebook account no longer active. Falling through the cracks.

I have ceased to be.

§

Jim   I resort to begging. I turn up at her flat and shout outside the window and cry on her door.

Lucy   I want to ring someone to get rid of him but there's no one to ring.

Jim   I tell her that I'm not leaving.

Lucy   So we arrange to meet.

Jim   She agrees to meet me.

Lucy   And the idea of seeing him. I don't know what will happen to me.

§

Jim *starts to do some sit-ups. He can barely manage two.*

He does some press-ups. He struggles. It's a little desperate.

Lucy *starts to dress. She looks down at her body in disgust. She quickly covers herself.*

Jim *pulls out his shoes. They are beaten up and scruffy. He spits on them. Tries to polish them with his sleeve.*

Lucy *struggles to zip up her dress by herself.*

Jim   I hope that I have the right words to say.

Lucy   I hope that I don't crumble.

Jim   So I say I'm sorry.

(*To* **Lucy**.) I'm so sorry.

Lucy   And we are to go for dinner. By the river.

He looks so smart. And he's so delicate with me. Opens the door for me. Looks at me. Every last inch of me.

Takes in every word I say as if it were the most important thing in the world.

And I think about telling him.

Jim *takes up a seat.*

Lucy *sits opposite* **Jim**.

Lucy   I look into those eyes. They're like another world. Sparkling sea.

I think I should tell him. Want so badly to tell him what he could be.

Jim   And she looks so beautiful. Why didn't I tell her every day how beautiful she was? Why didn't I tell her that she is responsible for every bit of happiness I've experienced in my adult life?

Lucy   And I missed someone looking at me the way he does.

Jim   Her smell washes right over me again. And being here. Looking at her. Holding her hand. I just want to freeze and not say or think another word because I'm so happy . . .

Lucy   I start to think what it might be like to kiss him again.

Jim   All I want to do is take her face in my hands and kiss her again.

Lucy   I have to stop myself from leaning over the table and kissing him again.

Jim   But does she even want me to kiss her again?

I can't ruin this. I have to get this. Right.

Lucy   I want him to take me in his arms and tell me that everything is going to be alright.

Jim *reaches across and takes* **Lucy** *by the hand.*

Lucy   I imagine he could be a father . . . I imagine that . . .

I should tell him.

She recoils from **Jim**'s *hand.*

Jim   It's the way she's looking at me.

I don't deserve her at all.

And I can see the pain behind her eyes. I did that. It was my fault.

And a wave of disgust rushes all over me. I hate what I did to her.

Lucy   And he's not looking at me again. His eyes are falling to the floor.

Jim   I should say something. Tell her that I have thought about her every second of every day. But she needs more than that. She deserves more than that.

Lucy   Was it something I said? Something that I did?

Jim   I wish she wouldn't look at me like . . .

I wish . . . I wish . . .

Lucy *rushes away to her room.*

§

Jim   She runs out of the restaurant and I follow after her.

Lucy   I wanted him to follow me.

Jim   But I know. I know.

Lucy   I ask him to come home with me.

Jim   That she is gone from me for ever.

Lucy   But I can't let go of him. I loved him. With all of me.

Jim *slowly enters* **Lucy***'s room.*

Jim   I am in her room again. In her flat. I am with her. And she is with me.

Lucy   I wonder if I let him hold me, that everything will be alright?

Jim *kisses* **Lucy***, she starts to cry.*

He is trying not to cry.

They kiss more and more. It grows more passionate. It's kind, apologetic, caring, and it's sad.

They have sex slowly and gently, never leaving one another's gaze.

They stop having sex. They embrace.

Jim *removes himself from* **Lucy***'s arms. He goes to leave. He stops to look at her one last time.*

§

Jim   I know that I was a fool. I know that I was a coward. I know I had no idea that my world was in her eyes.

I'm really sorry. I don't think I can say any more.

Please don't look at me like that.

I don't know if . . .

Please . . .

I wonder what she does every second of the day. I wonder if she is having the time of her life. I wonder if the city is her playground all over again?

Lucy   I'm at a clinic.

Hello! magazines on a cheap white coffee table. A sixteen-year-old girl and a terrified boyfriend and a steely-looking mum. A bully of a man who is arguing with his crying Eastern European girlfriend. And me. On my own.

Jim   Because she had a life before me. Happy pictures on a wall. A life.

Lucy   A nurse takes me upstairs and a doctor asks me lots of personal questions. Including the most personal of all.

Why?

I tell him that we're no longer together. He asks me if the baby is the reason. Which I think is a bit too personal but it makes me slightly angry. Which means I don't cry. For now.

He gives me a pill. And a glass of water.

It's young enough to take a pill. It's not really a 'thing' at all.

He tells me it will all happen in twenty-four hours.

§

Jim   I see her getting dressed in the morning.

Lucy *takes a tablet.*

Jim   And walking to work with her paper coffee cup in her hand.

I see her on a train. I see her at work. I see her smile. That smile. My God. That smile. Wow. Wow. Wow.

Lucy   They said the pain would be like a period.

Jim   And then I think of the pain I caused her. And it tears me apart.

Lucy   It's agony.

Her legs buckle. She clings to her stomach. A shrilling moan of agony.

I am being punished for this.

Jim   I see her everywhere.

Lucy *is on the floor, in extreme pain. Clutches her stomach.*

Jim   I wait for her to call. Please call.

Lucy *howls in pain.*

Jim   It's as if she's dead. But this is much worse than grief.

Lucy   Agony. Agony. Agony.

Jim   I walk through the Portrait Gallery and sob in the silent halls.

Lucy *staggers to her feet.*

Lucy   I have to move on, you see.

Start again.

Jim   Tony tells me to move forward. But Tony is an idiot.

And all I can do is cling to every tiny memory. It makes me happy for a time.

Happy there. Happy then.

Lucy   Because I can't be like this. In the city.

She doubles up in pain.

Got to work. Got to live. Got to . . .

She staggers. She is gradually recovering now. She looks up into a bright light.

Enough now.

It hurts too much.

§

Jim   Thinking about moving back to Mum and Dad's for a bit. Collect myself.

He starts to cry.

Lucy   I was hoping you could help me.

Jim   I miss her. I miss her. I miss her. I.

Lucy   I am alone.

Jim   I miss her. I miss her. I miss her.

Lucy   And you're supposed to tell me now.

Jim   I was hoping you could help me.

Lucy   How I can stop forward again.

Jim   Because I'm falling through the cracks.

Lucy   I thought you could help me.

Jim   Help me. Help me. Help me.

Lucy *sings the second verse of 'Save Me'.*[1]

Lights.

---

[1] Words and music by Brian May.

Bloomsbury Methuen Drama Modern Plays
include work by

Bola Agbaje
Edward Albee
Davey Anderson
Jean Anouilh
John Arden
Peter Barnes
Sebastian Barry
Alistair Beaton
Brendan Behan
Edward Bond
William Boyd
Bertolt Brecht
Howard Brenton
Amelia Bullmore
Anthony Burgess
Leo Butler
Jim Cartwright
Lolita Chakrabarti
Caryl Churchill
Lucinda Coxon
Curious Directive
Nick Darke
Shelagh Delaney
Ishy Din
Claire Dowie
David Edgar
David Eldridge
Dario Fo
Michael Frayn
John Godber
Paul Godfrey
James Graham
David Greig
John Guare
Mark Haddon
Peter Handke
David Harrower
Jonathan Harvey
Iain Heggie

Robert Holman
Caroline Horton
Terry Johnson
Sarah Kane
Barrie Keeffe
Doug Lucie
Anders Lustgarten
David Mamet
Patrick Marber
Martin McDonagh
Arthur Miller
D. C. Moore
Tom Murphy
Phyllis Nagy
Anthony Neilson
Peter Nichols
Joe Orton
Joe Penhall
Luigi Pirandello
Stephen Poliakoff
Lucy Prebble
Peter Quilter
Mark Ravenhill
Philip Ridley
Willy Russell
Jean-Paul Sartre
Sam Shepard
Martin Sherman
Wole Soyinka
Simon Stephens
Peter Straughan
Kate Tempest
Theatre Workshop
Judy Upton
Timberlake Wertenbaker
Roy Williams
Snoo Wilson
Frances Ya-Chu Cowhig
Benjamin Zephaniah

Bloomsbury Methuen Drama Contemporary Dramatists

include

John Arden (two volumes)
Arden & D'Arcy
Peter Barnes (three volumes)
Sebastian Barry
Mike Bartlett
Dermot Bolger
Edward Bond (eight volumes)
Howard Brenton (two volumes)
Leo Butler
Richard Cameron
Jim Cartwright
Caryl Churchill (two volumes)
Complicite
Sarah Daniels (two volumes)
Nick Darke
David Edgar (three volumes)
David Eldridge (two volumes)
Ben Elton
Per Olov Enquist
Dario Fo (two volumes)
Michael Frayn (four volumes)
John Godber (four volumes)
Paul Godfrey
James Graham
David Greig
John Guare
Lee Hall (two volumes)
Katori Hall
Peter Handke
Jonathan Harvey (two volumes)
Iain Heggie
Israel Horovitz
Declan Hughes
Terry Johnson (three volumes)
Sarah Kane
Barrie Keeffe
Bernard-Marie Koltès (two volumes)
Franz Xaver Kroetz
Kwame Kwei-Armah
David Lan
Bryony Lavery
Deborah Levy
Doug Lucie

David Mamet (four volumes)
Patrick Marber
Martin McDonagh
Duncan McLean
David Mercer (two volumes)
Anthony Minghella (two volumes)
Tom Murphy (six volumes)
Phyllis Nagy
Anthony Neilson (two volumes)
Peter Nichol (two volumes)
Philip Osment
Gary Owen
Louise Page
Stewart Parker (two volumes)
Joe Penhall (two volumes)
Stephen Poliakoff (three volumes)
David Rabe (two volumes)
Mark Ravenhill (three volumes)
Christina Reid
Philip Ridley (two volumes)
Willy Russell
Eric-Emmanuel Schmitt
Ntozake Shange
Sam Shepard (two volumes)
Martin Sherman (two volumes)
Christopher Shinn
Joshua Sobel
Wole Soyinka (two volumes)
Simon Stephens (three volumes)
Shelagh Stephenson
David Storey (three volumes)
C. P. Taylor
Sue Townsend
Judy Upton
Michel Vinaver (two volumes)
Arnold Wesker (two volumes)
Peter Whelan
Michael Wilcox
Roy Williams (four volumes)
David Williamson
Snoo Wilson (two volumes)
David Wood (two volumes)
Victoria Wood

For a complete catalogue
of Bloomsbury Methuen Drama
titles write to:

Bloomsbury Methuen Drama
Bloomsbury Publishing Plc
50 Bedford Square
London WC1B 3DP

or you can visit our website at:
www.bloomsbury.com/drama

Printed in Great Britain
by Amazon